MILLION DOLLAR INSPECTOR

Your Proven BLUEPRINT to Unlock Hidden Fortunes in a $100 Billion Market

Peter Van de Sande

Copyright © 2025

Peter Van de Sande, Author

Published by Named by Design Publishing

www.namedbydesign.com

ISBN: 978-0-9862712-8-1

Edited by: Marni MacRae

All Rights Reserved.

No part of this book may be reproduced, stored in a retrieval system, or transmitted by any means, electronically, mechanically, or via photocopying, recording, or otherwise, without written permission from the author,
Peter Van de Sande.

This book is for educational purposes only. The author does not guarantee specific results. Always consult qualified professionals regarding career or financial decisions.

First Edition

TABLE OF CONTENTS

Introduction: Million-Dollar Mirage- What You've Been Chasing Is An Illusion 1

Chapter One: Million-Dollar Enigma -Unseen Industry...................... 4

Chapter Two: Million- Dollar -Prism Seeing What Others Don't . 14

Chapter Three: Million-Dollar Grit-Unteachable Advantage 30

Chapter Four: Million-Dollar Threshold-Where The Truth Starts And Excuses End 39

Chapter Five: Million-Dollar Decoy-Fraud. Fakes. False Signals .. 47

Chapter Six: Million-Dollar Arsenal- Your Presence. Your Image. Your Edge 56

Chapter Seven: Million-Dollar Ignition-The Spark. Launching Transformation 64

Chapter Eight: Million-Dollar-Ripple What You Leave Behind Brings You Back 74

Chapter Nine: Million-Dollar Portal Step -Through or Stay Stuck.....85

Final Words – From All Fields To All Futures 97

INTRODUCTION

MILLION-DOLLAR MIRAGE WHAT YOU'VE BEEN CHASING IS AN ILLUSION

They told you to get a degree.

They told you to play it safe.

They told you to follow the crowd and hope for security at the end of a paycheck.

But **they never told you this**: That an entire industry, worth over **four hundred billion dollars**, has been operating behind the scenes, funding careers, feeding fortunes, and building quiet empires for those trained to see it.

This isn't home inspection.

This isn't flipping houses or real estate speculation.

This is something overlooked… and far more powerful.

We're talking about the **inspector economy**—the professionals sent to verify assets, protect investments, expose fraud, assess risk, and unlock funding across every major sector:

- Commercial property
- Corporate lending
- Residential insurance
- Retail compliance
- Equipment verification
- Disaster and damage assessment

While the world scrolls, posts, and hustles for digital likes, **inspectors are in the field, quietly getting paid.**

Not chasing trends.

Not building followers.

Building wealth.

And most people have never even heard of them.

This book was written to change that.

Inside, you'll meet everyday men and women who went from overlooked to overbooked—simply by getting trained, certified, and prepared for a career almost no one is talking about… yet.

They didn't have a license.

They didn't have experience.

What they had was a blueprint **and the courage to follow it.**

Now it's your turn.

You've found the door they never told you existed.

The only question is: **Will you step through it... or let it close and go back to scrolling?**

CHAPTER ONE

MILLION-DOLLAR ENIGMA- UNSEEN INDUSTRY. A PUZZLE HIDING IN PLAIN SIGHT.

Shocking Truth

Right now, as you're reading this, thousands of people are earning six figures, some even seven, without a college degree, without a warehouse full of inventory, and without a storefront or social media following. They're not influencers. They're not salespeople. And they're not tech geniuses.

They're inspectors.

Not home inspectors.

They're specialized, highly trained field inspectors operating in one of the most misunderstood and overlooked sectors of the modern economy. You've likely passed one of them at a gas station, in line at a coffee shop, or even sitting quietly in the corner of a bank lobby, clipboard or tablet in hand. You didn't know it, but you were looking at someone earning a fortune in one of America's hidden industries.

You Weren't Supposed to Know About This

This isn't a career path that gets advertised on job boards or talked about at career fairs. It's not taught in school, and no one's guiding you toward it, because, frankly, most people in this industry don't want the competition.

For over four decades, I've trained men and women to step into this hidden world. I've watched former waiters, security guards, teachers, and veterans build six- and seven-figure incomes in record time, because once you learn how to spot the opportunity, you'll realize you've been surrounded by it all along.

But why is it hidden?

Because too many people still believe that wealth must come from traditional routes; college degrees, corporate ladders, or startup ventures. But when you look behind the curtain, you'll see something shocking: Industries like insurance, finance, asset management, and real estate are quietly dependent on a specialized workforce they rarely talk about. And that's where the goldmine lies.

While the world chases real estate flips, tech startups, and side hustles that fizzle out, a quiet empire has been growing behind the scenes:

- Commercial buildings
- Mortgage-backed assets
- Insurance portfolios
- Corporate compliance
- Environmental risks
- Retail and restaurant chains
- National disaster response
- Government contracts

Every one of these industries depends on **trained, certified inspectors** to verify, document, and assess, often before the public even knows there's a problem.

And here's the kicker: There are **hundreds of niches**, but **ninety percent of inspectors only touch three of them.**

That means opportunity isn't just available, it's wide open for those with the right training and insight. The gatekeepers won't advertise it. Schools won't guide you to it. But that doesn't mean it's not real.

Most people spend their whole lives walking past doors they never knew could open.

Now you know.

The Numbers They Don't Teach You in School

Let's talk numbers:

- The U.S. field services inspection industry is part of a **four hundred billion-dollar** market.

- Mortgage inspections, occupancy verifications, insurance condition reports, equipment verifications, asset checks—these are just some of the inspections happening across the country every single day.

- A properly trained field inspector can complete three to six jobs a day at seventy-five dollars to two hundred and fifty dollars per job, with almost no overhead.

- Some elite inspectors are earning **three to seven hundred thousand dollars a year**, completely independently, working by choice, not by clock.

- Master inspectors can earn upwards of **seven hundred thousand dollars** a year.

These are real numbers. I've trained the people behind them. And yet, most people don't even know this is a *thing*, begging the question: why?

Why You've Never Heard This Before

Because no one profits when you figure it out. Not the colleges, not the corporate world, not the broken job placement system.

The truth is, inspection work doesn't require thousands in student loans, a four-year degree, or climbing someone else's ladder. It requires skill, professionalism, training, and access to a system that works.

You've been conditioned to chase prestige and predictability. But the people quietly winning? They chased opportunity and results. They found an industry nobody talks about but everyone needs.

And once they saw it, they never looked back.

Meet The Quiet Professionals Who Are Quietly Winning

Let me introduce you to a few individuals I've personally trained, people who didn't come from flashy careers or privileged paths. They came with determination, got trained, and discovered the goldmine hiding in plain sight.

Ross – From Fast Food to $250K+ Leadership

When I first met Ross, he was doing maintenance at a McDonald's. He was humble, hardworking, and overlooked, just like most people in that kind of job. But Ross had something more important than a résumé: He had drive. He stepped into the training program, put in the work, and within nine months became a **loss control consultant** for a long-term health care facility, pulling in **seventy-five thousand dollars a year.**

That would've been enough for some. But not Ross.

He continued leveling up, adding certifications, building his field knowledge, mastering risk analysis, and not long after, he landed a **director's position** overseeing inspections and compliance for one of the most elite preparatory academies in the country. Today, Ross earns upwards of **two hundred and fifty thousand dollars a year**, proving that it's not where you start, it's whether or not you see the opening in front of you.

Tim – The Remodeler Who Reinvented His Role

Tim had been in construction for years, remodeling homes, flipping the occasional property, but his income had plateaued. He was tired of the feast-or-famine cycle and needed a smarter, more sustainable path.

After training, Tim saw what others missed: **He was already walking onto job sites with inspection potential.** So, he added residential insurance inspections to his service offerings, providing insurance high-value inspections, exterior hazard surveys, and site and sketch for the same clients who once only needed drywall or framing.

It didn't take long before Tim's inspection side work grew into a core business. He now earns a consistent **six-figure income**, and the best part? He works fewer hours with higher pay and far less physical wear and tear.

Sarah – From Inexperienced to in-Demand

Sarah was a single mom with no background in inspections or insurance. She came into the program not with experience but with purpose. She showed up, stayed late, asked questions, and never stopped learning.

Six months later, Sarah was offered a position with **one of the top three insurance companies in the United States** as a full-time in-house insurance inspector. This wasn't a temporary gig or a contract job. It was a **career-defining opportunity**, with benefits, stability, and excellent pay.

Sarah's story proves that even without prior experience, the right training can change your life. She didn't just get a job, she rose through grit and skill into a world where access is earned, not given. These aren't outliers. These are the kind of transformations that happen when you stop waiting for opportunity and learn how to inspect it.

These are the million-dollar inspectors. And this book will show you how to become one.

You're Looking at the Hidden Entry Point to a Four Hundred Billion-Dollar Market

This is the beginning of your shift.

You're not reading this by accident. You've found your way to a door that opens into a market almost nobody sees, but funds and supports nearly every major financial transaction in this country. It touches everything from mortgage lending to fleet leasing and insurance underwriting.

And the gateway to it all? **Inspections.**

Not in a lab. Not in a house. But in the real world, where contracts are verified, risks are managed, and assets are assessed by inspectors like you *could* be.

This industry isn't declining, it's expanding. And there's room for those with the right mindset and the right preparation.

Million-Dollar Move (Action Step)

Now it's your turn.

Million-Dollar Move #1: Identify your blind spot.

What beliefs have you held about work, income, or success that may no longer serve you?

Right now, write down three assumptions you've had about earning a high income, and question those assumptions. Where did those beliefs come from? Are they still true? Are they keeping you blind to opportunities?

You cannot seize a future you're not willing to see.

This chapter was meant to open your eyes. Next, you'll find out how to stop watching from the sidelines and start building your future.

Welcome to the start of your million-dollar path.

CHAPTER TWO –

MILLION-DOLLAR PRISM- SEEING WHAT OTHERS DON'T

Shocking Truth:

Untrained inspectors are quietly costing U.S. companies over **five billion** dollars a year through missed red flags, incomplete documentation, overlooked liabilities, and bad photos.

That's not just poor performance, that's **expensive negligence**.

Certified inspectors, on the other hand, are not just observers. They conduct **critical, high-stakes evaluations**, scrutinizing vehicles, properties, and facilities to uncover:

- Hidden damages
- Fraudulent activity
- Liability exposures

- Crucial compliance issues

These findings often prevent lawsuits, stop fraud in its tracks, and help clients make informed, educated decisions with confidence.

In the inspection industry, timely service is of the utmost importance because delays can derail transactions, jeopardize compliance, or even put lives at risk.

The difference between a routine report and an expert analysis? **Millions in savings or millions in losses.**

Not All Inspectors Are Created Equal

At a glance, inspection work may seem straightforward, just a four-step task:

1. Show up
2. Take photos
3. Fill out a form
4. Submit the report

But that's the **form-filler mindset**, and it's exactly why so many inspectors are being **phased out**. They do the bare minimum, miss crucial details, and fail to meet today's rising standards for procedure, accuracy, and professionalism.

Elite inspectors, however, operate by the **Million-Dollar Standard,** a methodical, client-focused process that demonstrates precision, preparation, and professionalism at every step.

This isn't a four-step task, it's a **16-step system** that transforms an ordinary task into a high-value service.

The Million-Dollar Inspector Process:

1. Call the contact in advance

2. Ask key questions to clarify scope

3. Schedule and confirm inspection time

4. Review job order for accuracy and completeness

5. Ensure you have the correct inspection-specific forms

6. Prepare and pack a fully equipped inspector toolkit

7. Locate the property or business site accurately

8. Confirm correct address upon arrival

9. Make a professional, confident introduction to the contact

10. Strategically plan your inspection approach

11. Take comprehensive, high-quality photos

12. Record detailed notes during inspection

13. Conduct a final interview with the contact to clarify or confirm findings

14. Call client for real-time report clearance

15. Contact company to give update

16. Complete report using both visuals and written analysis

The difference? One inspector checks boxes, the other **builds trust, secures contracts**, and becomes **irreplaceable.**

Let's break down the difference.

Side-by-Side Comparison: Untrained vs. Million-Dollar Inspector

Category	Untrained Inspector	Million-Dollar Inspector (MILLIONS Standard)
Mindset	"Get it done. Move on to the	**M – Mastery:** Intentionality, excellence,

Category	Untrained Inspector	Million-Dollar Inspector (MILLIONS Standard)
	next."	continuous improvement
Preparation	Minimal. Brings a clipboard.	**I – Integrity**: Factual, honest, and fully prepared with tools and research
Client Interaction	Unclear. Reactive. Timid.	**L – Leverage**: Builds rapport with contact, client, and company
On-Site Actions	Snaps photos. Rushes. Misses details.	**L – Leadership**: Proactive, takes initiative, owns the inspection outcome
Documentation	Short, vague notes. Basic checkboxes.	**I – Irreplaceable**: Impeccable reports, sharp photos, and thorough analysis

Category	Untrained Inspector	Million-Dollar Inspector (MILLIONS Standard)
Professionalism	Casual attire. Uncertain conduct.	**O – Openings**: Seizes the moment, presents like a trusted consultant
Post-Inspection	Submits and disappears.	**N – Never Say No**: Answers every call, builds every bridge, becomes essential
Value & Perception	Anyone can do the job.	**S – Set Apart**: Knows their worth, owns their role, and delivers unmatched value

Case Study: Same Job, Two Outcomes

Leased Equipment Inspection – Medical Billing Office | Six-Hour Emergency Assignment

A leasing company needed answers fast. A medical billing firm had applied for financing tied to twenty leased computers. The inspector had just six hours to verify serial numbers and complete the report. On the surface, it looked routine.

But nothing about this job was ordinary. And only one inspector saw it for what it truly was.

Inspector A – The Untrained, Box-Checker

- **Approach:** Arrived and let the office contact read serial numbers aloud, no verification beyond the surface.

- **Findings:** Noted two serial numbers didn't match. Simply updated them.

- **Observations:** Only one person onsite. Tiny office space. No questions asked.

- **Report Submitted:** Basic checklist. Minimal details. No red flags raised.

Result:

Funding was approved. Two weeks later, the "business" was gone. All twenty computers vanished. The leasing company took a five-figure loss. The inspector? Never called again.

Inspector B – The Certified, Trained Professional

(True Story – Author's Personal Account)

- **Initial Clue:** A 1,000 sq. ft. office divided into three sections. Supposedly housing twenty active workstations, but only one employee in sight.

- **Red Flag #1:** The Contact wouldn't let him verify the equipment directly. Claimed there was no room to walk through, so he read serial numbers aloud.

- **Red Flag #2:** Two computers didn't match the lease: different serial numbers, different brands, different models.

- **Red Flag #3:** No staff present. No noise. No visible operations. Nothing about the site matched a functioning business.

The MILLIONS Method in Action

- **M – Mastery:** Does this operation make any logical sense? No.

- **I – Integrity:** Truth above task. Report what's real, not what's requested.

- **L – Leverage:** Ask critical questions others avoid.

- **L – Leadership:** Take initiative. Investigate beyond the clipboard.

- **I – Irreplaceable:** Delivered a detailed report with flagged risks, photo evidence, and expert insight.

- **O – Openings:** Recognized diversion tactics. Followed the inconsistencies.

- **N – Never Say No:** Used authority to dig deeper, even under time pressure.

- **S – Set Apart:** What action would you take if this were your money?

Action Taken:

Immediately after leaving the site, the inspector called the leasing company to give phone clearance, advising them to pause funding immediately based on critical discrepancies and a high probability of fraud.

Conclusion:

Two weeks later, the business had vanished. The location was empty. All twenty computers were gone.

But the money wasn't. The leasing company had halted the deal just in time.

Final Result:

The inspector was officially recognized for saving the company tens of thousands in potential losses. He was requested by name for all future inspections. His inspector rank increased. His fee structure changed.

He didn't just complete a job, he became irreplaceable.

The Million-Dollar Difference:

➢ The untrained inspector filled out a form.
➢ The Million-Dollar Inspector protected an entire finance portfolio.

Why Certification is the Competitive Edge

Companies don't just buy reports, they buy **protection, compliance, accuracy,** and **peace of mind.**

This was proven in the story above: An untrained inspector would have cost the client thousands.

A Million-Dollar inspector saved the client and became irreplaceable.

In today's industry, the demand is shifting:

Not for box-checkers but for critical thinkers.

Not for warm bodies but for certified professionals who see what others miss.

What Certified Inspectors Deliver (That Others Don't)

1. Business-Level Awareness

- They understand risk, liability, compliance, and financial exposure.
- They know how to protect their clients.

2. Industry-Specific Communication

- ➢ They speak the language of underwriters, lenders, facility managers, and adjusters.
- ➢ They build trust fast with contacts, companies, and clients.

3. Reports That Matter

- ➢ More than photos and checklists, they offer insight, red flags, and clear recommendations.
- ➢ Their documentation prevents losses, flags fraud, and reduces risk.

5. Professionalism at Every Step

- ➢ From attire to attitude, their presence reinforces reliability and trust.
- ➢ Their consistency sets the standard others are measured by.

The Steps to Certification and Success

Want to stand out? Here's how certified inspectors prepare, think, and work differently:

Step 1: Understand the Mission

Before even stepping on-site, certified inspectors review the job specifics, client goals, and time service.

Step 2: Prepare Like a Pro

They know what tools are required: measuring wheel, ladder, additional forms, batteries, and always have them available.

They mentally rehearse the job, ensuring no detail is overlooked.

Step 3: Show Up as the Expert

They dress to be trusted, are on time, have a positive attitude, and are professional.

They are ready to interview, assess, document, and lead.

Step 4: Communicate Like a Consultant

They don't "send" reports—they deliver insight.

They provide phone clearance, updates, and appreciation that deepens client loyalty.

Step 5: Deliver More Than Expected

Their reports are clear, actionable, and thorough.

They don't just do the job, they become the *go-to* inspector the client requests by name.

The Career Shift Certification Creates

This is how you go from:

Gig worker → Trusted ally

Chasing gigs → Selecting clients

One-time job → Ongoing inspection

Interchangeable → Irreplaceable

Certification doesn't just teach you how to inspect, it trains you how to **think, communicate,** and **operate** like the professional clients can't afford to lose.

This is what separates a basic inspector from a million-dollar inspector.

Million-Dollar Move (Action Step)

Use the MILLIONS Method as your on-site mental checklist every time.

Before submitting your next report, stop and run through this quick but powerful filter:

M – Mastery: Did I fully understand the scope and context, or did I just follow instructions?

I – Integrity: Did I report what's *true*, even if it's uncomfortable or inconvenient?

L – Leverage: Did I use client interaction to gather deeper insight, not just surface answers?

L – Leadership: Did I take initiative on-site or wait for someone to tell me what to do?

I – Irreplaceable: Will my report make the client say, "We need this inspector again"?

O – Openings: Did I spot hidden risks, inconsistencies, or red flags others might miss?

N – Never Say No: Did I go the extra step, even when the task was "complete"?

S – Set Apart: If this were *my* money, *my* risk, did I act accordingly?

This is your edge. Most inspectors submit photos. You submit insight, foresight, and professional clarity.

Million-Dollar Inspectors don't just finish jobs, they filter every move through MILLIONS.

Next Step: Print this method. Tape it inside your toolkit. **Live it until it's instinct.** That's how trust is built and how empires are made.

CHAPTER THREE

MILLION-DOLLAR GRIT- UNTEACHABLE ADVANTAGE

Shocking Truth:

In an industry worth over **four hundred billion dollars**, a single inspector's judgment can influence multi-million-dollar transactions, determine liability, or expose fraud. Yet most companies don't fire inspectors for lacking knowledge, they stop using them for lacking **character**.

This is not a job for the passive.

This is not a field for the fainthearted.

And this is definitely not for anyone who's "just looking to make a quick buck."

But for the right person? This industry is the most **profitable, liberating, and trusted role** you'll ever step into.

The Million-Dollar Misunderstanding

The most common question we hear is: "What experience do I need to become a certified professional inspector?"

But that's not the question that matters. The better question is:

"Do I have the **traits** that make someone *unstoppable* in this field?"

Because here's the truth:

- You can teach someone how to complete a form.
- You can train someone to use tools.
- You can memorize standards and pass certifications.

But what you **can't fake** is:

- Integrity
- Judgment
- Discipline
- Professionalism
- Critical thinking under pressure

Traits are what separate the average inspector from the one who gets called again and again.

Who This Industry is Not For

Let's be blunt: **Not everyone is built for this.**

This industry is **not** for:

- People who look for shortcuts
- People who crack under pressure
- People who fear accountability
- People who can't manage time or deadlines
- People who wait for permission
- People who devalue ethics for convenience

Inspectors are entrusted to **validate, document, and protect** real assets, insurance funds, commercial properties, mortgage investments, and corporate portfolios.

If you're not ready to carry that weight with precision and pride… this is not your lane.

The Core Traits of a Million-Dollar Inspector

These aren't just soft skills. These are **hardened characteristics** that show up in every elite, certified inspector, and they align directly with the **MILLIONS Method.**

M – Mastery

Trait: *Detail-Driven Focus*

Million-Dollar Inspectors don't "wing it." They master the scope, the standards, and the stakes—before stepping foot on-site. They study. They prepare. They become fluent in their field.

Mastery means you're never guessing, and that certainty earns trust.

I – Integrity

Trait: *Unshakable Honesty*

You'll be alone in the buildings, trusted with access, paid to report the truth, even when it's uncomfortable. Million-dollar inspectors don't omit, exaggerate, or sugarcoat.

Professional inspectors don't take shortcuts. They take **responsibility.**

L – Leverage

Trait: *Situational Awareness + Human Insight*

Elite inspectors don't just assess property, they read people. They build rapport with gatekeepers, extract vital details, and represent the client with professionalism and tact.

They know how to **ask the right questions** and uncover what others miss.

L – Leadership

Trait: *Initiative Under Pressure*

When plans change, access is denied, or something seems "off," they adapt. They don't wait for instructions. They take ownership and lead the process with poise and problem-solving.

They're **on-site decision-makers.**

I – Irreplaceable

Trait: *Unmatched Professionalism*

From proper attire to polished reports, they bring excellence to every interaction. Clients don't see them as interchangeable; they see them as **essential.**

Their work speaks volumes. Their presence sets the bar.

O – Openings

Trait: *Analytical Thinking + Curiosity*

They know that fraud hides in plain sight. They follow inconsistencies. They probe when something doesn't make sense. They don't assume, they investigate.

Where others stop at what's obvious, they dig for what's true.

N – Never Say No

Trait: *Discipline + Ownership*

No task is beneath them. No detail is "too small." No job gets checked off without pride. They finish strong, even when it's hard, hot, late, or inconvenient.

The elite inspector's name becomes **synonymous with dependability.**

S – Set Apart

Trait: *Client-Centric Mindset*

They treat every assignment like the stakes are personal, because they are. If the roles were reversed, they ask:

"Would I trust this report if my money were on the line?"

Set-apart inspectors **protect reputations and portfolios**, not just complete tasks.

Example:

Scenario: The "Waterlogged Warehouse" Lie

After a major hurricane swept through the Gulf Coast, a CAT adjuster was dispatched to inspect a large commercial warehouse reported as a "total loss due to flooding." The owner claimed the entire inventory, high-end electronics, was destroyed, filing a multimillion-dollar claim.

But the adjuster noticed inconsistencies:

- The waterlines on the drywall didn't match the reported flood level.

- The packaging on the remaining boxes was suspiciously dry.

- Security camera systems had been "inoperable due to the storm." There was no interior or exterior video footage.

Digging deeper, the adjuster discovered that the actual cause of damage was not due to the flooding from the hurricane but instead due to a broken pipe in the bathroom, and the water was never shut off. He was able to make this determination by observing and documenting the water level and the broken pipe.

Outcome: The claim was denied. Legal charges were filed for insurance fraud. The adjuster's sharp eye and willingness to go beyond the checklist saved the carrier millions and revealed a coordinated scam.

If You See These Traits in Yourself… You're Already Ahead

You might not have the certification yet.

You might not know the terminology.

You might not own a clipboard.

But if these traits describe you, **you're already miles ahead of the average inspector.**

And if you're not there yet? Good news:

Traits can be strengthened through discipline, training, and mentorship.

That's what this program is built to do.

Million-Dollar Move (Action Step)

Use the MILLIONS Method (above) to evaluate yourself right now:

1. **Circle three traits you already demonstrate.**
2. **Underline two traits that need growth.**
3. **Choose one trait to develop with intensity over the next thirty days.**

Every contract, every referral, every opportunity in this industry flows through trust. And trust begins with who you are, not just what you do.

In this business, **character is currency**. And you're about to become rich.

CHAPTER FOUR

MILLION-DOLLAR THRESHOLD- WHERE THE TRUTH STARTS AND EXCUSES END

Shocking Truth:

Despite a hundred billion dollars invested in AI surveillance, drone imaging, and virtual monitoring technologies over the last five years, **insurance fraud has increased by over twenty-six percent**, because algorithms can't assess intent. They can't verify claims. And they definitely can't do an interior inspection and interview the homeowner.

Only one thing has proven effective in stopping risk at the door: an inspector who has deductive reasoning, critical thinking, and keen observational skills.

When you walk a property, the entire decision-making process depends on what you see, capture, question, and report.

You're not just there, you're *the reason* truth is found.

In a World of Litigation, Risk, and Fraud – Truth is Currency

Corporations, lenders, government agencies, and insurers are all navigating an increasingly hostile landscape. Today's reality includes:

- Soaring litigation tied to property conditions
- Multi-layered regulatory audits
- Skyrocketing occupancy and leasing fraud
- Hidden environmental liabilities
- Disputed insurance claims on a massive scale
- Billions lost annually in misrepresented data

What's missing?

A reliable, unbiased witness who shows up, walks the site, and says:

"Here's what's really happening."

That's not a drone's job. That's not AI's domain. **That's you.**

Why Companies Need *You*—Not a Camera, Drone, or Algorithm

AI can flag anomalies.

Drones can take top-down photos.

Virtual agents can autofill forms.

But they can't replace what your senses, judgment, and presence can detect:

- **Hazardous** adjacent exposures
- A **safety hazard** tucked just out of frame
- The **hesitation in a voice** that reveals deception
- Wrong building **classification**
- A "vacant" property with **fresh tire marks** and **furnishings**

AI detects patterns. You detect problems. And when money, liability, or lives are on the line, **that difference matters.**

You Are Non-Vested, And That Changes Everything

Companies can't rely on internal staff or contacts (homeowner, business owner, insurance agent) to report accurately. They come with baggage: pressure, conflict of interest, and agenda.

You, on the other hand, are:

- Certified

- Unaffiliated

- Objective

- Trained to observe without bias

- Paid to report facts, not feelings

You don't promote. You don't persuade. You **protect** clients, portfolios, reputations, and legal outcomes.

In an age of misinformation, your *unbiased truth* is the most valuable service a company can buy.

The Human Factor is the Game-Changer

AI can't feel tension in a room.

AI can't follow a gut instinct.

AI can't ask a follow-up question based on intuition.

Only a real human, standing on the ground, reading the energy in a room, **can catch the difference between a technical truth and a deceptive reality.**

You're not a data collector, you're a decision enabler. When you walk the site, you change what happens next.

The Inspector is the Missing Piece in High-Stakes Decision Making

Your documentation might be the tipping point between:

- **Approving** a multi-million-dollar commercial loan or stopping fraud in its tracks
- **Paying** an insurance claim or launching an investigation
- **Opening** a new location or shutting down a fire trap
- **Verifying** a lease or protecting a national chain from environmental liability

You're not "doing a job," you're delivering **undeniable evidence** that helps clients **move forward with legal and financial clarity.**

Why the Demand for Field Inspectors is Skyrocketing

➢ **Over forty-eight percent rise** in mortgage fraud investigations since 2020

- **Over thirty-five percent increase** in commercial site inspections after a disaster
  - **Over seven billion dollars** paid out in fraudulent insurance claims in 2024 alone

What's driving the need?

- Insurers require **real-time verification** before payout
- Mortgage companies demand **proof of occupancy and condition**
- Retailers need **code compliance and safety validation** before expansion
- Government agencies are outsourcing **field inspections** for disaster response, environmental hazards, and regulatory compliance
- Property managers need **third-party documentation** to settle tenant disputes

Every one of them needs a person. Not a program.

Real-Life Example:

The Report That Saved Millions

Carol, a certified inspector trained through our elite program, was assigned to verify minor roof damage after a warehouse fire.

When she arrived, her inspection instincts kicked in.

Instead of just snapping photos of the roof, she toured the interior, noting watermarks, sagging ceiling panels, and a damp odor inconsistent with fire-related damage.

Her findings revealed **deep internal structural rot** that had existed long before the fire, and had nothing to do with the claim.

Her report, complete with time-stamped photo evidence and on-site inspection report, saved the insurance company over $1.2 million.

That's the power of **human judgment.** That's the role only *you* can play.

Why AI Can't Replace You (And Never Will)

Let's be clear:

- AI doesn't know the feel of a soft and sagging floorboard
- Drones can't interpret body language

- Satellites won't question a leaseholder's vague answers
- Remote inspections can be manipulated
- Automated forms can be forged
- But trained inspectors: Ask the second question
    - Walk the extra ten feet
    - Stay until the full story is clear
    - Document reality, not theory
    - Stand between clients and catastrophic mistakes

You are the **truth filter** in a world full of noise.

Million-Dollar Move (Action Step)

Next time you walk a site, remind yourself of this truth:

"I'm not here to complete a task, I'm here to protect people, money, and decisions."

Now write this down: **"I am the eyes, ears, and integrity of the decision-making process."**

Repeat that before every inspection, then go prove it, because *no AI can replace what you bring.*

CHAPTER FIVE

MILLION-DOLLAR DECOY- FRAUD. FAKES. FALSE SIGNALS

Shocking Truth:

Fraud is no longer the exception. It's becoming the expectation.

The global economy loses more than **five trillion** dollars every year to fraud, more than the entire GDP of Japan. In the U.S. alone:

- **Mortgage fraud** has jumped **over forty percent** in the last five years.
- **Insurance fraud** costs businesses **$308 billion annually**.
- **Occupancy fraud** has tripled since 2020, and many lenders don't even know it's happening until after they've lost the asset.

- **Falsified inspections** and **staged properties** are flooding both residential and commercial sectors.

And enforcement?

It's underfunded, reactive, and often shows up *after* the damage is done.

Which is why certified, boots-on-the-ground inspectors are no longer optional. **They're essential.**

Fraud isn't Just a Crime – It's a Crisis

Fraud wears many masks, and most of them look convincing on paper.

Across industries, it's creeping into inspection reports, photos, documentation, and exaggerated property conditions. Here's where it's hiding:

- **Mortgage & Banking:** Fake occupancy, falsified signatures, manipulated photos, shell tenants
- **Insurance Claims:** Inflated damage, old damage claimed as new, unpermitted work
- **Commercial Leases:** Misrepresented square footage, sublets without disclosure, non-compliant tenants

➤ **Construction & Renovation:** Phony timelines, counterfeit materials, misappropriation of funding

Inspectors are not law enforcement, but they are the **first and best chance** at uncovering the truth before fraud becomes fallout.

The Inspector as the Unpaid Investigator

You're not just documenting a site, you're verifying reality.

Your presence disrupts fraud by doing what no camera or AI can: **Recognizing patterns, spotting deception, and asking the right questions.**

Common real-world red flags you might see:

- A flooded basement "recently repaired" with no visible pump or invoice
- A brand-new fire extinguisher tag with a fake inspection date
- Photos in a report that match a different building altogether
- Equipment on-site that doesn't match the lease agreement

You're not there to accuse, you're there to observe.

And your documentation becomes the client's most powerful defense.

Why Fraud Detection Makes You Invaluable

Most companies aren't equipped to detect fraud. Their employees are:

- Too close to the deal
- Too eager to close
- Too trusting of documents
- Too distant from the site

They need you, the trained, neutral third-party who sees with **unbiased clarity** and reports with **precision**. Every inspection is turned into a legal document.

Your report can become:

- The reason a fraudulent claim is denied
- The key document in a court case
- The trigger for an internal audit
- The signal that prevents a six- or seven-figure loss

Your camera doesn't just capture images, it captures the truth.

Your presence doesn't just check boxes, it blocks fraud.

Scenario: The Fireplace That Exposed Fraud

Gene, a certified Million-Dollar Inspector, was dispatched to complete a routine **property status report** on a foreclosed home marked "vacant."

At first glance, everything seemed to match the vacant classification:

- Driveway scattered with unopened newspapers
- Blinds tightly shut
- Lights off inside

But Gene didn't just scan the scene, he *read* it. That's when he noticed something unusual:

Thin wisps of smoke curling from the chimney.

Most would've missed it. Gene didn't.

He followed the clues:

- A **back door left unsecured**

- A **trash can in the yard filled with fresh food containers**
- And clear signs of **recent occupancy**, despite the property being listed as empty

He didn't wait.

Gene returned to his vehicle and initiated an **immediate phone clearance** with the mortgage company, reporting that the property was being illegally subletted.

The result? The mortgage company called the local sheriff's department to investigate.

Gene's report didn't just protect one asset, it exposed a broader fraud pattern in the region.

Within weeks, Gene was offered an exclusive contract to handle all property status inspections statewide.

That single moment of due diligence didn't just earn respect, it earned him the ability to retire a few years later, financially secure.

This is the power of trained instincts.

This is what it means to be a Million-Dollar Inspector.

Fraud Grows in Silence—Inspectors Break That Silence

Fraud flourishes where no one's looking.

Where everyone assumes.

Where paperwork goes unchecked.

Where images are manipulated.

Where no one walks the site, listens, smells, questions, or verifies.

You break that silence.

- You walk where others guess.
- You photograph what others skip.
- You document what others ignore.
- You stay when others would've already left.

You don't just close the file. **You close the loophole.**

The True Cost of Fraud—Across Key Industries

Industry	Estimated Annual Losses	Common Inspection-Related Fraud
Insurance	$308 Billion	Exaggerated damage, false claims, staged loss

Industry	Estimated Annual Losses	Common Inspection-Related Fraud
Mortgage & Lending	$15 Billion	Occupancy misrepresentation, fake income
Commercial Leasing	$10 Billion+	Square footage fraud, illegal subletting
Construction & Renovation	$12 Billion	Phantom labor, reused photos, unpermitted work

These numbers don't lie, but **people do**.

That's why inspectors are the last and best line of defense.

Million-Dollar Move (Action Step)

Start thinking like a **fraud detector**, not just an inspector.

Next time you're on-site, go beyond the checklist. Ask yourself:

- Does this match what I was told or what's on the equipment invoice?
- Is this property telling a different story than the paperwork?
- Am I being guided away from certain areas or questions on purpose?

Fraud survives where questions go unasked.

Be the one who asks. Be the one who verifies.

Be the reason it doesn't happen on your watch.

CHAPTER SIX

MILLION-DOLLAR ARSENAL- YOUR PRESENCE. YOUR IMAGE. YOUR EDGE

Shocking Truth:

In the inspection industry, clients decide whether to trust you within the first thirty seconds of meeting you. That trust isn't built solely by your report, it's forged by your presence, your preparedness, and your professionalism on site. When you're equipped and ready, you can save millions by catching fraud, mitigating risks, and ensuring that every detail counts.

Sixty-eight percent of inspectors who are removed from a company's rotation are dismissed due to poor appearance, lack of preparedness, unprofessional behavior, and inspection mistakes.

In fact, a 2023 field services report revealed that **one in four clients will reject a report outright** if the inspector appeared disorganized, had problematic photos, or failed to provide phone updates.

In this industry, trust is visual before it's factual.

And when you look unprepared, you *are* unprepared in the client's eyes.

Why Inspectors Are Getting Dropped – Even When the Report Is "Correct"

1. The Rise of the "Gig Mentality"

Over the past decade, the inspection industry has seen an influx of independent contractors treating inspection work like gig apps, similar to food delivery or ridesharing.

- Many enter the field with little understanding of what's at stake.
- They approach it as a short-term side hustle, not a professional role.
- As a result, they show up **underprepared, underdressed, and mentally disengaged.**

The client sees the difference immediately, and trust evaporates before the first photo is taken.

2. Low Barrier to Entry = Low Standards (At First Glance)

Some inspection platforms and subcontractors make it easy to accept jobs without proper training, tools, or oversight. This gives the illusion that "anyone can do it," which leads to:

- Poorly equipped inspectors showing up at multi-million-dollar properties
- Missed details, incomplete documentation, or sloppy interactions
- Contacts questioning whether the inspector is legitimate

When an inspector shows up in jeans, is ill-prepared, or fumbles over the purpose of the visit, it reflects directly on the client's brand and liability.

3. Disconnect Between Pay and Perception

Because many inspectors are paid per job (not hourly or salaried), they often underestimate the **value of presentation, preparation, and communication**, focusing only on completing tasks quickly.

- The mindset becomes *"Just get it done."*

- But clients think, *"Do I trust this person's judgment?"*

The work may pay like a gig, but the **consequences play out in court.** Clients need inspectors who understand that.

4. Inspection = Liability Control

Banks, insurers, and asset managers aren't hiring inspectors just to take photos. They're hiring them to:

- Detect fraud
- Prevent loss
- Confirm compliance
- Shield from lawsuits

If an inspector **looks unprofessional or untrustworthy**, it immediately undermines the credibility of the inspection, even if the report is accurate.

Many contracts are lost not because the inspector made a mistake but because they didn't inspire confidence.

Bottom Line:

In this industry, how you show up *is* part of the inspection.

Official documents, a collared shirt, and a confident introduction is not "extra." That's the minimum standard for a trusted, elite inspector.

Excellence isn't an Accident—It's a Choice

Million-dollar inspectors don't just show up. They show up prepared, polished, and professional every time. That edge comes from three pillars: the right equipment, the right etiquette, and the right mindset. This chapter breaks down what separates a "report-filler" from a trusted authority in the field, from the contents of your toolkit to the tone of your voice.

1. Equipment: What Every Inspector Carries

A top-tier inspector's gear isn't just a random collection of tools; it's a carefully assembled mobile office built for precision, reliability, and trust. While the exact tools you carry may vary depending on the type of inspection, your toolkit should always include the essentials needed for the specific jobs you take on. The goal is simple: Be prepared for every site, every time.

2. Etiquette: Professionalism in Every Detail

Clients aren't just hiring your tools, they're hiring a reflection of their own brand, standards, and risk mitigation practices.

The way you present yourself, speak, and interact sets the tone for the entire engagement.

- ✓ **Dress the Part**
- ✓ **Speak with Confidence and Clarity**
- ✓ **Stay Neutral, Stay Sharp**

Your appearance, tone, and communication shape client trust and build your professional reputation as an unstoppable, detail-oriented inspector.

3. Excellence: The Role of Critical Thinking

A Million-Dollar Inspector doesn't just follow a checklist, they think critically and see what others miss. Your mindset transforms raw data into actionable intelligence. Ask yourself:

- **Does this situation match the location's recorded details?**
- **What photos are needed to paint an accurate description?**
- **Does it make Sense?**

That's how you move beyond taking pictures; your critical thinking ensures that every discrepancy is documented, every anomaly is recorded, and every observation stands up under scrutiny.

Real-World Thinking in Action

- Noticing **paper tags for serial numbers** that don't match up.
- Observing a **different business name on signage** than what appears on the inspection form.
- Recognizing when **equipment isn't operating as expected.**

This is the level of attention that elevates you from a task-oriented technician to a trusted expert whose reports can thoroughly influence multi-million-dollar decisions.

Scenario: The Power of Preparedness

Luis, an inspector in professional attire, arrived at his first commercial site visit fully equipped with his complete toolkit, a clipboard, and a calm, confident demeanor. When he met the property manager, she said:

"Here is the rent roll you asked for. I knew when you asked for this last night on our phone call, and now seeing you in person, you really know what you're doing."

Though the job took only thirty minutes, Luis's preparedness, appearance, and professionalism not only impressed the client but also secured him a multi-city portfolio of over forty retail site inspections, an opportunity that would define his career.

Million-Dollar Move (Action Step)

Audit your gear, your attire, and your language. Ask yourself:

- **Am I dressed like an expert consultant?**
- **Do I carry the tools that ensure I am efficient, effective, and thorough to get the job done correctly?**
- **Do I speak and write with the clarity and professionalism that instills immediate trust, even on phone clearances and providing updates?**

Because in this business, the way you show up becomes your brand. Million-Dollar inspectors own the room the moment they arrive, and they're the difference between a mediocre report and a career-defining one.

CHAPTER SEVEN

MILLION-DOLLAR IGNITION- THE SPARK. LAUNCHING TRANSFORMATION

Shocking Insight:

Less than **five percent of field inspectors** hold any training beyond entry-level certification. Yet those who pursue master training and inspector certification **earn ten times more**, land long-term contracts, and are viewed as **trusted consultants**, not task-runners.

But here's the cost of that imbalance: Every year, **billions of dollars are lost** because of **untrained or undertrained inspectors**. And worse, every error, oversight, and missed fraud doesn't just cost money... It damages the reputation of the entire industry.

When Inspectors Aren't Trained, Everyone Pays

Poorly trained inspectors don't just make small mistakes; they create **systemic risk**. They miss fraud. They skip over hazards. They fail to flag legal issues that lead to:

- Delayed claims
- Denied loans
- Litigated leases
- Multi-million-dollar losses

And when that happens, **clients lose trust not just in one inspector but in the entire inspection process.**

Untrained inspectors:

- Cost companies money
- Cost clients their confidence
- Cost this industry its credibility

The damage of one inaccurate report can ripple across entire portfolios, resulting in lawsuits, asset forfeiture, and crushed reputations.

The Rising Demand for Certified, Elite, and Master Inspectors

The nature of the inspection industry has changed. We're no longer in a world of clipboard-walkthroughs and generic reports.

Today's clients, banks, insurance carriers, REITs, private equity firms, national retailers, and government agencies aren't just looking for basic inspections. They expect excellence. They demand:

- Ironclad documentation that holds up under legal and regulatory scrutiny
- A verified inspection portfolio that proves professional training and certification
- Fluency in industry-specific language and reporting standards
- Comprehensive protection of their investments and physical assets
- Risk mitigation that limits liability and financial exposure
- Precise, reliable data to drive confident, informed decisions
- High-quality, professional photographs that capture and communicate the full reality of the situation

And the demand is rising fast.

Some of the Industries Now Requiring Professional Inspectors:

- **Insurance Loss Control** (PCA, risk mitigation, and safety and hazard exposures)
- **Commercial Real Estate** (multi-family properties, retail centers, and office buildings)
- **Mortgage Servicing** (occupancy verification, foreclosure/bankruptcy inspections, and collections)
- **Retail Expansion & Rollouts** (pre-leasing inspections, merchant verifications, and general site evaluations)
- **Healthcare & Long-Term Care Facilities** (state/federal audits, compliance reviews)
- **Auto Dealerships** (AIM, repossession audits, collateral verification, and condition reports)
- **Equipment Leasing** (restaurant, heavy equipment, and office)
- **Construction** (pre/post-funding, draw, site evaluations)

Most training programs fall short because they're narrowly focused, designed only to teach company-specific forms, checklists, and internal procedures. They don't prepare inspectors to meet the elite, industry-wide standards that top-tier clients demand.

This creates a critical gap: Inspectors may know how to follow one company's system, but they lack the versatility, credibility, and professional rigor required to succeed across industries, contracts, and high-stakes environments.

Million-dollar inspectors solve this.

Million-dollar training goes beyond the basics. It instills the gold standard of inspection excellence, training inspectors to think critically, document professionally, speak the language of the industry, and operate at a level that earns trust from national and global clients.

It's not just about knowing a form, it's about becoming the inspector that companies *fight* to hire.

The Power of the Inspection Portfolio

In a world flooded with applicants and underqualified inspectors, *credibility* is currency, and your inspection portfolio is the proof of your worth.

A million-dollar inspection portfolio is more than a resume, it's a performance record.

It showcases real-world inspections the professional has completed in their specific area of certification, including residential, commercial, insurance loss control, or specialty inspections. Each file demonstrates the inspector's ability to meet strict documentation requirements, adhere to legal and industry standards, and communicate findings clearly and visually.

This portfolio is a *proof of concept* living document that says, "I've been trained. I've delivered. And here's the evidence."

The Bottom Line

In an industry valued at over **four hundred billion dollars**, inspectors who can *prove their performance* don't chase jobs; they attract them.

Million-dollar inspectors are trained to build and maintain a portfolio that becomes a career multiplier. It's the difference between a job seeker and a sought-after professional. And in today's climate of liability, accuracy, and documentation, that difference is everything.

From Paycheck to Prestige: The Million-Dollar Inspector Effect

Tina was stuck.

Twelve years in retail had drained her, with long hours, little recognition, and no clear path forward. She wasn't licensed, didn't have inspection experience, and wasn't even sure she could start over.

But she *knew* she wanted out.

That's when she found the **Million-Dollar Inspector Certification Program** and made a decision that would change everything.

Within just four months of completing her training:

- She landed a **managerial role with a Fortune 500 loss control firm**
- Her **starting salary exceeded a hundred thousand dollars**, instantly doubling her income
- She was given a **company car**, a **full expense account**, and even a **golf club membership**—not for play, but to **build high-level client relationships**

What made her stand out?

Her **elite-level certification**, her **professional-grade portfolio**, and her ability to **speak the language of liability, risk, and asset protection**, all skills she gained through Million-Dollar Inspection training.

She didn't enter the industry as just another contractor. She walked in as a **trained authority**; polished, credible, and client-ready.

Tina didn't just land a job, she stepped into a new identity. From overlooked to in-demand. From retail burnout to respected leader.

And it all started the day she chose to train.

Million-Dollar Move (Action Step): From No Experience to Industry-Ready

If you're new to the industry, with no license, no background, and no prior experience, **you're not behind. You're right on time.**

The truth? Most inspectors start without a roadmap. But Million-Dollar Inspector gives you more than just information, we give you **real-world experience that builds your confidence and your credibility**.

During your training, you won't just study inspections, you'll **conduct them.**

You'll walk through real assignments, document real findings, and assemble a **professional-grade inspection portfolio** that proves what you're capable of from day one.

This is what sets million-dollar inspectors apart:

- **You get hands-on experience before your first job.**
- **You build a portfolio while you learn, not after.**
- **You enter the field prepared, polished, and positioned to succeed at a high level.**

Ask yourself:

- Am I ready to move from uncertain to unstoppable?
- Am I willing to learn, apply, and grow into a career that's built on trust and results?
- Am I ready to stop doubting and start building something that lasts?

You don't need a background in inspections. You just need a beginning, and **this is it.** Certification doesn't just change what you earn, **it changes what you believe is possible.**

And with Million-Dollar Inspector, you won't just hope you're ready—**you'll know you are.**

CHAPTER EIGHT

MILLION-DOLLAR RIPPLE- WHAT YOU LEAVE BEHIND BRINGS YOU BACK

Shocking Insight

In a world built on precision, the greatest failures aren't caused by missed measurements, they're caused by missed connections.

"Across the broader inspection industry, poor communication and weak client relationships are responsible for up to sixty-five percent of contract losses, missed renewals, and reassignments, costing individual inspectors and firms tens of millions annually."

Supporting Insights:

- **Loss of Repeat Work:** According to industry reports from facilities compliance, insurance inspections, and commercial evaluations, many contracts are not renewed, **not because of poor technical performance** but because **inspectors failed to communicate clearly, deliver results professionally, or build rapport** with clients and field managers.

- Industry insights suggest that **lapses in communication and failure to build rapport are leading reasons contractors stop receiving assignments** in third-party inspector networks, such as those involved in retail audits and field verifications. *Insight:* This emphasizes the importance of consistent communication and relationship management for inspectors to secure repeat assignments.

- In industries like insurance, mortgage lending, and commercial compliance, **client retention has a direct impact on profitability.** According to *Glassbox*, increasing customer retention rates by just five percent can boost profits by twenty-five percent to ninety-five percent. Additionally, *TotalExpert* reports that acquiring a new customer can cost five to twenty-five times more than retaining an existing one.

The Ripple Effect:

Poor communication doesn't just cost the job, it **costs referrals, second-tier contracts, multi-state accounts, and the inspector's reputation across an entire network.** The inspection may be silent, but success is loud, and success requires connection.

Most inspectors enter the field thinking success comes from knowing how to fill out a form or take a few photos. But **million-dollar inspectors** know better.

In this industry, it's not just what you do, it's how you connect.

You can be trained. You can be skilled. But if you can't build trust across all levels of the inspection process, **you'll never rise above average**.

That's why **Leverage**, the "L" in the MILLIONS Method, is not just a tactic, it's a principle for life.

In the inspection world, **leveraging relationships is how you multiply trust, credibility, income, and opportunity.**

The Three Relationship Pillars

Every successful inspection rests on **three essential relationships**. Ignore them, and you remain forgettable.

Leverage them, and you become irreplaceable.

1. Company

The company is the inspection company that hires you to represent them. They are your gateway into high-value work and long-term contracts.

These companies serve powerful clients, banks, insurance carriers, REITs, and financial institutions. When you represent the company well, you're not just completing a task, you're **strengthening a reputation**, earning trust, and becoming the go-to name on every job request.

Leverage means protecting and elevating the company brand, because their success becomes your success.

2. Contact

The contact is the individual at the inspection site who gives you access, answers questions, and may even accompany you during the inspection process. This could be a store manager, property owner, on-site supervisor, or policy holder.

Many inspectors treat the contact as an afterthought, just someone to open a door.

But million-dollar inspectors know: **The way you treat the contact can open future doors.**

Leverage here means showing respect, asking intelligent questions, maintaining professionalism, and leaving an impression. They often report back to the company or even the client, and your reputation begins right there, on-site.

3. Client

The client is the financial institution, insurance carrier, or corporate entity that ordered and is paying for the inspection. You may never meet them face-to-face, but **they are always watching** through your reports, photos, and performance.

And in many cases, you *do* speak with them, especially during **phone clearances from the site**. That call isn't just a formality, it's your spotlight.

Your tone, your knowledge, your ability to clearly and confidently communicate, **that's where reputations are built.** That's when clients say, *"We want that inspector again."*

Author's Story: Christmas Eve, a Cement Mixer, and the Power of Leverage

After months of performing high-dollar collateral verifications for a top-tier financial institution, I was assigned a last-minute inspection on **Christmas Eve.**

The assignment: Exchange a check for **forty-five thousand dollars** in return for the title to a 2004 cement mixer truck.

Time was critical. The location? **Seventy-five miles from my home.**

I confirmed the business was open, drove to the site, and got to work: photos, VIN verification, odometer reading. But when I reviewed the title, I noticed a critical issue: **The VIN was missing one digit.**

The owner admitted the error was known, but as per protocol, I couldn't release the check without **clearance.**

Here's where training kicks in and relationships matter.

I immediately called **my inspection company**, but their office had closed early for the holiday.

Most inspectors would've left the property and driven home. But I had built a **relationship with the client,** the financial institution that issued the check.

I called **Ann, the title manager**. Thankfully, she hadn't left yet. I explained the situation. She authorized me to release the check and documented her approval on the phone log.

I then left a **voicemail for my company**, logging the date, time, and Ann's exact instructions, including every detail.

The contact on-site was relieved and grateful. Unknown to me, he later called the **client** to praise the professionalism and resolution I provided.

Three weeks later, I was performing another inspection for that same client. During the required phone clearance, the person on the other end paused and said: *"The president would like to speak with you."*

What he told me changed everything: "In all our years of working with inspectors, you stand out. Your photos, your report writing, and most of all—the way you build rapport during phone clearances. From now on, we've formally requested that only **you** handle all inspections in your region."

That moment wasn't about a form or a photo. It was about the **Company. Contact. Client.** And how each relationship, when leveraged with excellence, builds not just a reputation but a career.

The Takeaway

Most inspectors think they're in the business of data collection.

You're in the business of trust-building.

Forms fade. Reports get filed away. But **relationships are remembered.**

Company. Contact. Client.

Master those three, and you'll never have to chase contracts again; **they'll chase you.**

And yes, it affects your wallet. Because people don't hire the inspector who filled out the form. They hire the one who went the extra mile, picked up the phone, and proved they could be trusted.

Signature Training Spotlight: The Lost Language of Connection

Why Relationships Aren't Just a Soft Skill, They're the Key to Everything

The Christmas Eve inspection wasn't remarkable because of a truck or a title. It stood out because of the *human factors* most inspectors never train for:

- A frustrated contact onsite
- A closed office line
- A client who could've been unreachable
- A decision that had to be made in real-time, under pressure

It was trust, built over months, that got the check released.

It was clear communication that kept the deal from collapsing.

It was rapport earned one phone call at a time that made a financial institution president request your name on every job going forward.

This is what most training programs miss.

They teach the forms. They skip the follow-through.

They cover procedures. They ignore people.

That's why we developed our signature training:

The Lost Language of Connection

Because inspectors today aren't failing on the form, they're falling short in the field **when it comes to people.**

What You'll Learn:

- How to manage tense moments with professionalism and empathy
- How to speak with authority on phone clearances and earn instant trust
- How to leave a lasting impression on contacts who influence future work
- How to document real-time communication with precision and clarity
- How to create loyalty with clients, even if you never meet them in person

Why This Matters

In an industry full of checklists and automation, it's easy to forget:

People don't refer paperwork. They refer people.

The inspector who can connect is the one who gets remembered and requested.

Not because they did the job, but they knew how to build trust at every level of the process.

If you've ever felt unprepared for an uncomfortable interaction, if you've ever walked away thinking, *"I should have handled that better,"* then you already know **this training is for you.**

Because the skill you never thought you needed **might just be the one that builds your million-dollar career.**

CHAPTER NINE

MILLION-DOLLAR PORTAL-
STEP THROUGH OR STAY STUCK

One path gives you a paycheck, the other builds your legacy.

But both require one thing: **a decision made now.**

Shocking Insight: This is the Moment Most People Miss

Let's be real: **Over ninety percent of people who come across a life-changing opening don't fail because it's too hard; they fail because they wait.**

They hesitate.

They talk themselves out of it.

They promise they'll come back to it... and never do.

And that's where their story ends.

Success doesn't slip away, it gets claimed by someone who moved faster.

Right now, the **more than four hundred billion-dollar inspection industry** is wide open.

The opportunity is real. The demand is rising. The blueprint is in your hands.

But here's the truth: **If you don't move, someone else will.**

And the contracts, the income, the career you've been hoping for? They'll belong to the person who acted when you paused.

So, ask yourself, **will this be the moment you remember or the one you regret?**

You've seen what's possible. Now it's time to decide:

Are you in, or are you going to let it pass you by?

There's a moment that comes for all of us.

It doesn't knock. It doesn't wait. It just appears—quiet, unspectacular, and dares us to move.

Most people miss it. Not because they didn't see it but because they **paused.**

According to a global regret study, eighty-three percent of people say their biggest life regret isn't something they did, it's something they didn't do.

A chance they didn't take. A door they didn't walk through.

A decision they delayed… until it disappeared.

James and Deanna were both standing in that moment. No experience. No connections. No guarantees. Just a clear opportunity… and a choice.

James hesitated.

He got excited. Highlighted some lines. Bookmarked the page. He said he'd "think about it."

That night, he watched Netflix instead. Next week, work got busy. Time marched on, and he forgot about it.

Now that James is older, he thinks about what could have been.

Deanna didn't wait.

She felt the nudge and moved. She enrolled **that same day**. She didn't have it all figured out, but she took the next step.

Ten weeks later, she was certified.

By month six, she was conducting **high-dollar commercial inspections**.

By year two? She cleared **a hundred and eighty thousand dollars**, hired a team, and never looked back.

Same opportunity. Same moment. **Two different reactions.**

Two entirely different lives.

So, the only question now is: **When this moment passes... will you be James or Deanna?**

Because you'll remember this moment. The only question is, **will you remember it with pride... or regret?**

The Crossroads: Employee or Entrepreneur?

Now that you've seen the blueprint, there's one final decision to make: Will you take the **structured route** or blaze the **ownership path**?

Option 1: The Employee Route—Predictable, but Capped

You become an employee with an established firm. They assign you the work, they define your duties, and they structure your hours.

Pros:

- Stable Income
- Paid Vacation
- Additional Benefits

Cons:

- Set Income
- Rigid work environment
- No ownership

Ideal For:

- Beginners who want field experience
- Those seeking lower risk and higher structure
- Individuals who want to learn before launching

Option 2: The Entrepreneur Route—Riskier but Unlimited

- You don't just earn a living, you design a life that's meaningful, profitable, and fully yours.

Pros:

- Unlimited earning potential
- Flexible scheduling
- Multiple clients

Cons:

- Assume full financial responsibility
- Unpredictable Income
- No Company Benefits

Ideal For:

- Visionaries with ambition
- Professionals ready to own their future
- Those seeking a high level of success

Million-Dollar Master™—The Final Tier of Inspection Excellence

Becoming a **Million-Dollar Master™** means you're no longer just an inspector; you're a force in the industry. You've earned certifications across multiple high-value sectors, built a portfolio that commands attention, and proven you can lead, consult, and execute at the highest level. You're not tied to one niche, you move between them with confidence and clarity.

You don't follow the standard, you set it.

This isn't just a title**, it's the mark of mastery.** And more than that... **This is how you make yourself irreplaceable.**

When clients, companies, and contracts demand the best, they don't just want someone certified, they want a **Million-Dollar Master™**.

The Cross-Trained Advantage: The True Path to Master Status

If you want to become a **Million-Dollar Master™ Inspector**, don't just learn one slice of the industry; **master the full scope.**

The highest-paid, most in-demand inspectors aren't specialists stuck in one lane. They're **cross-trained professionals**, certified and fluent in the three most powerful verticals of the inspection world:

- **Residential Risk & Insurance Inspections**
- **Commercial Compliance & Loss Control**
- **Specialty & Strategic Inspections** like Retail Surveys, Equipment Verification, or Disaster Recovery

They don't just "do inspections," **they understand the entire system, and that's why they claim a position of influence.**

Why Cross-Training Works:

- You're never dependent on one niche, one season, or one type of client

- You can pivot when markets shift and pick up contracts where others can't
- You speak the language of multiple sectors, giving you a strategic edge
- You gain access to *more opportunities, better clients, and higher fees*

This is how Million-Dollar Master™ Inspectors are built: through training, certification, and total industry fluency.

It's not about hopping from job to job; it's about **becoming so valuable, so versatile, and so well-prepared** that clients can't afford to overlook you.

True success isn't found in one lane, it's in mastering the map.

Credibility-Driven Support:

- Inspectors trained in **three or more specialties** are **four times more likely** to receive ongoing direct contract work than single-focus inspectors.
  Source: Industry employment data and contractor reports
- Cross-certified inspectors command **thirty-five to sixty percent higher average fees** due to their flexibility and strategic insight.

Source: Contractor Payment Index / Insurance Risk Network

- Over **eighty-five percent** of Million-Dollar Inspector **graduates** who reached six-figure earnings did so by getting certified in multiple verticals.

Bottom Line:

If you want to stand out in a competitive, four-hundred-billion-dollar industry, you need to know it from the inside out.

Cross-training is not optional; it's the foundation of a career that pays, lasts, and leads.

Success Has a Deadline –Will You Miss It Again?

Let's be honest, if "playing it safe" worked, **you wouldn't still be searching.**

Have you:

- Jumped from job to job, hoping one would finally pay what you're worth?
- Tried building a business that never scaled or never even started?

- Watched others pass you by and wondered, *What do they know that I don't?*

This book just told you.

The only question now is: **Will you act or will you watch it pass you by again?**

Shocking Insight:

The inspection industry is undergoing a massive transformation, driven by technology, regulation, and explosive demand.

Over sixty percent of top inspection firms say they can't find enough certified inspectors to meet demand.

Source: National Field Services Benchmark Report, 2024

Meanwhile, the market is expanding fast: The U.S. inspection services industry surpassed **four hundred billion dollars** in 2024 and is projected to grow **fifteen percent annually** through 2028.

Source: IBISWorld & Allied Market Research

That means thousands of high-paying contracts are up for grabs right now.

But here's what most people don't realize: **According to a global behavior study, eighty-three percent of people say their biggest regret in life is not taking action when they had the chance.**

They didn't fail because they weren't capable. They failed because they hesitated.

Every Week You Wait:

- Clients are awarding contracts to certified pros
- Niches are being filled by faster movers
- Inspectors with less experience but more action are landing the jobs you hoped for
- The barrier to entry grows, not because the door is closed,

but because someone else already walked through it

The Bottom Line:

The longer you wait, the more you'll wish you hadn't. Because this isn't just a career opportunity, **it may be the greatest financial decision of your life.**

So ask yourself... **Will this be the moment you finally make a move** or the one you *always look back on* with regret?

Final Million-Dollar Move (Your Next Step):

If you're still reading, **you're ready.**

Not someday. **Today.**

The path is proven. The training is essential. The future is yours.

Go to www.MillionDollarInspector.com and begin your transformation today.

This is your Million-Dollar moment. Seize the opening now.

FINAL WORDS – FROM ALL FIELDS TO ALL FUTURES

From a Single Vision to a Standard That Changed Everything

What began in 2002 as *All Fields Training* wasn't just a school but a vision. We believe ordinary people become unstoppable when equipped with the right training, uncompromising standards, and fearless leadership.

That vision became a legacy of excellence through Michelle Van de Sande, innovator and wife of author Peter Van de Sande. With over **forty years of teaching experience** across every educational level, from pre-kindergarten to college and university, Michelle brought unmatched depth to the training process. She holds a master's degree in curriculum and instruction, earned the prestigious Master Teacher Designation, and is an award-winning author who has trained and transformed the lives of hundreds of thousands across education and business sectors.

Together, her academic expertise and Peter's real-world mastery forged a curriculum built not just to educate but to unlock potential, rewrite futures, and produce leaders.

Million-Dollar Method. Million-Dollar Training. One Outcome: The Million-Dollar Inspector.